IRISH FAMILY NAMES

RYAN
Ó MAOILRIAIN

IRISH FAMILY NAMES

RYAN
Ó MAOILRIAIN

Dáithí Ó hÓgáin

GILL & MACMILLAN

Published In Ireland by
Gill & Macmillan Ltd
Hume Avenue, Park West
Dublin 12
with associated companies throughout the world
www.gillmacmillan.ie
Text © Salamander Books 2003
0 7171 3556 X

Published by arrangement with Salamander Books Ltd, London

A member of **Chrysalis** Books plc

A CIP catalogue record is available for this book from the British Library.

9 8 7 6 5 4 3 2 1

All correspondence concerning the content of this volume should be addressed to
Salamander Books Ltd.

THE AUTHOR

Dáithí Ó hÓgáin, MA, PhD, is Associate Professor at University College Dublin,
Ireland, where he lectures on Irish folklore. He is the author of over 20 books,
several of them in Irish, on aspects of folk culture, history and tradition. He is also
a noted poet and short-story writer, and is a well-known conference lecturer. He
has participated in the production of documentary films in Europe and the United
States, and is a frequent TV and radio broadcaster.

CREDITS

Project Manager: Stella Caldwell
Design: Q2A Solutions
Picture Research: Julie McMahon
Cover Design: Cara Hamilton
Colour reproduction: Anorax, UK
Printed and bound in Italy

Special thanks to Antony Shaw for his invaluable advice and generous assistance in
writing the section on modern members of the family.

CONTENTS

INTRODUCTION

THE HISTORY OF IRELAND IS

A GREAT DRAMA OF WAR,

INVASION, PLANTATION,

IMMIGRATION, EMIGRATION,

CONFLICT AND SOLIDARITY.

INTRODUCTION

Above: The entrance to the passage grave at Newgrange in County Meath is a fine example of Neolithic architecture.

People have been in Ireland for about 9,000 years but, for over two-thirds of that time, what they called themselves either as individuals or as groups is unknown. The Celticisation of Ireland had begun by the fifth century BC, and a few centuries later it was complete. This process must have involved the coming of some influential groups from Britain and perhaps from the Continental land-mass. The Irish language developed from the Celtic spoken by these, and all our earliest surviving system of naming—whether of people or of places—are in that language.

From references to the country in ancient Greek and Latin sources, and from the earliest written traditions of the Irish themselves, the names of important early population groups in the country can be postulated. Since the country was known to outsiders as Éveriu ('the land'), the fusion of indigenous peoples and early Celtic settlers was termed 'the land-dwellers' i.e. Éverini or 'Iverni'. Within these Iverni, the various groups had different names, most prominent being the Vinducati, Soborgii, Darinii and Uluti towards the north, the Ceuleni and Aucii on the east coast, the Gamarnates in the west, and the Autinii and Veldobri in the south.

A strong challenge to the Iverni soon presented

itself in the form of an amalgam of peoples in the broad area of the southern midlands, headed by a band of warriors belonging to the Brigantes of central Britain who had crossed the Irish Sea. The group became known as Leiquni ('casters'), a name which was reinterpreted as Lagini ('lance-men'). These Lagini seem to have coalesced at an early date with another group of incomers called Gaiso-lingi ('javelin-jumpers'), and together they extended their power over most of the south-eastern quarter of Ireland.

In the first century AD, new groups were arriving from Britain, escaping from the devastation caused by the Roman legions. These, such as the Dumnonii and Coriondi, joined with the Lagini, who began to threaten

Above: The Petrie Crown, an example of early Irish Celtic metalworking.

Left: Dún Eoghanachta, a massive ring fort on the island of Inishmore. Probably built in the fifth century, the fort takes it name from the Eoghanacht people who ruled most of Munster at this time.

Above: St. Patrick makes his way to the ritual centre of Tara some time in the fifth century.

the Ivernian kingdom of the north midlands. There are several indications that the prestigious ritual centre of Tara was seized from the Iverni by the Lagini in or about the second century. Meanwhile, in the south another group—with origins in south-west Britain or in Brittany—was building up a strong power-base. This was the Venii, who divided into two sections. One of these sections remained in the south, winning more and more territory from the Ivernian tribes there; while the other section moved northwards along the west bank of the Shannon and began to threaten the Lagini. By the early fifth century, they had crossed the Shannon and seized Tara, whom they pushed southwards beyond the river Boyne. Further migrations into Ireland were caused by the Roman campaigns against the north of Britain in the second and third centuries. The Celtic and Celticised peoples of that area were called Priteni ('painters'), which name was changed to Cruithni in Ireland. Reaching Ireland, these migrants settled in scattered groups in the north-east and on both sides of the Shannon.

From all of these groups are descended the Gaelic people of Ireland, with names developing into specifically Irish forms. For instance, the name of the country

Éveriu became Ériu and later still Éire, while the Iverni became Érainn. Strong groups among them kept their separate designations—especially the Uluti ('bearded men'), who became Ulaidh. For their part, the Lagini became Laighin, and the Cruithni became Cruithin. The Venii became Féni, with their southern section known as Eoghanacht and their northern section known as Connachta. This latter in time became the most powerful of all Irish septs, controlling the Boyne valley, as well as the large area west of the Shannon which still retains their name.

Ireland came to be considered as naturally divided into five parts, each part called a 'fifth' (cúige)—Ulaidh in the north; Connachta in the west; Midhe ('centre') comprising the north midland plain; Laighin in the south-east; and Mumhain ('the nurturing' i.e. domain of the land-goddess) in the south. Later in English these were known respectively as Ulster, Connacht, Meath, Leinster and Munster. Midhe as a provincial unit ceased to exist in the Middle Ages, and its territory is in fact part of the modern increased province of Leinster. This accounts for the four historic provinces of Ireland. In modern Irish, of course, the Irish people themselves are called Gaeil or Éireannaigh, and the inhabitants of the four provinces are called

Below: Dry stone cells constructed by monks on the island of Skellig Michael some time in the sixth century are perfectly preserved.

Above: A map of 1700 showing the Irish provinces of Ulster, Munster, Leinster and Connacht before the partition of Ireland.

respectively Ultaigh, Connachtaigh, Laighnigh and Muimhnigh.

Many Irish septs are still identifiable in the mediaeval period as descendants of the Érainn, Laighin, Connachta and Eoghanacht, and a lesser number of the Cruithin. These population groups had, however, developed into loose federations of kingdoms, ruled by strong extended families called *cineáil* ('septs'), each of which had a traditional septal name. A leader was referred to by his own personal name, and for clarity he was described as son of his named father. These simple patronymics gave way in the tenth and 11th centuries to habitual surnames of the type we now have. The septal names gradually came to be identified more with the territories inhabited by the septs than with the septs themselves.

In the year 795, the first Norse raiders appeared off the Irish coast, and within a generation or two they had progressed from being raiders to forming settlements. They set up some kingdoms inland, but those established by them on the sea-ports were more enduring. Despite the ebb and flow of almost incessant war in opposition to, and in alliance with different Irish septs, they remained an important force, with the Norse language being spoken in their settlements for several centuries. A considerable number of Irish surnames derive from the Norsemen, either by direct descent or by the interchange of culture.

The Normans, far-out cousins of the Irish Norsemen, conquered Ireland in the late 12th century, bringing with them Welsh, English, French and Flemish supporters. Within a century or two English became the dominant language among these settlers, but many of the chief Norman families in Ireland became strongly Gaelicised. They introduced a system of dividing the country into baronies, generally giving these baronies the names of the old septal territories. A large number of Irish surnames are of Norman extraction.

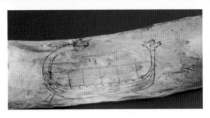

Above: Carving of a Norse ship.

The system of dividing Ireland into counties, each county comprising several baronies, dates from the reign of Queen Elizabeth I. Her successor, King James I, oversaw the Ulster Plantation, which brought in large numbers of settlers speaking Scottish Lallan, Scottish Gaelic and English. With the strengthening of rule from London, the English language gradually spread throughout the whole country and, with the widespread confiscation of land and its bestowal on settlers, many specifically English names entered the country. Most of these first names and some of the surnames developed Irish forms, but the contrary process was

Left: Norman ruins at sunset in Ballybunion, Co. Kerry.

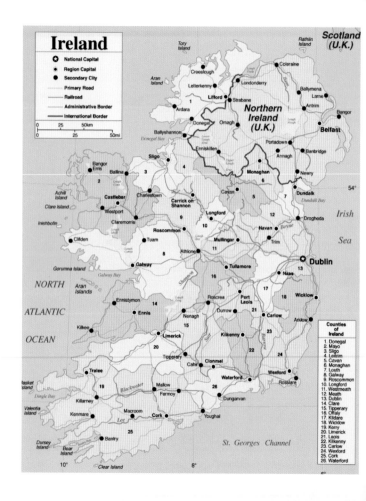

much stronger. Official versions of place-names were imposed in English, and anglicised forms of native Irish names were developed. It should be stressed that these anglicised forms, most prevalent in usage nowadays, are nearly all meaningless and give little indication of their derivation.

In Ireland there are numerous surnames of English, Scottish, Welsh, French, and other provenance. The histories of all these merit interest stretching beyond Ireland to their respective countries of origin. For general accounts of Irish surnames, see Edward MacLysaght, *Irish Families* (1957), *More Irish Families* (Dublin, 1960), *Supplement to Irish Families* (1964), and especially his *Surnames of Ireland* (1973). The last work contains a fine bibliography, as does Brian de Breffny, *Bibliography of Irish Family History and Genealogy* (1974). Further detail can be found in the many county and diocesan histories, as well as in learned journals which deal with historical and genealogical matters.

Argyle a muckle Scotch Knau in gude faith Sir.

Above: Satirical portrayal of Scottish Presbyterians who settled in Ulster during the 17th century.

Opposite page: A map of the modern counties of Ireland. The system of dividing Ireland into counties dates from the reign of Elizabeth I.

Left: A detail of the arms of the O'Malley family on the altar tomb in Clare Abbey.

TERRA MARIQ POTE
O·MAILLE

GENEALOGY

IRELAND'S DRAMATIC

HISTORY, LIKE ALL HISTORY,

IS COMPOSED OF COUNTLESS

INDIVIDUAL FAMILY

HISTORIES, EACH UNIQUE.

GENEALOGY

As we have shown, the Irish—like other nationalities—are in reality a worthy mixture of many different peoples. Genealogy can give but a tiny insight into our background, for the available information tends to be uneven, focusing mostly on people of social standing. The study of genealogy is an enjoyable pastime, but it should not involve any exclusiveness, for our dignity depends not on our descent but on our common humanity and individual personalities.

The first step in researching one's genealogy is to talk to relatives and friends, particularly elderly ones, and to note down all the information they have about the family tree. This ought to trace the tree back through two generations at least.

Documents pertaining to the household can also be of help, no matter how ephemeral they may seem. A journey to the local library comes next to see if members of the family are mentioned in any documents or publications there. One can also consult inscriptions on graveyard headstones where family members are known to be buried. Lists of old gravestone inscriptions for many counties are kept in the Genealogical Office (GO) and the National Archives of Ireland, Dublin (NAI), and others are published in local journals.

Several parts of Ireland now have local heritage centres, in which copies and indexes of many records, as well as published works, are kept. Information in these centres will have been selected from the range of

Above: Tracing your family tree is an enjoyable pastime. The first step is to talk to elderly relatives and friends, and note down any information they can offer.
Previous pages: The Book of the Boyles, showing the descent of the earls of Cork and Orrery.

surviving sources for the study of Irish genealogy, and
are listed here in general chronological order.

Earliest in date are the septal pedigrees—compiled
at various periods from the sixth century AD to the
Middle Ages. The prehistoric origins in these pedigrees
are partly fanciful, but otherwise they provide invaluable material. The texts have been assembled by
Michael A. O'Brien in *Corpus Genealogiarum Hiberniae*
(1962). Several mediaeval and post-mediaeval genealogies have been edited and compiled by John O'Donovan
—for whose work see R. I. Best, *Bibliography of Irish
Philology and of Printed Irish Literature*, vol. 1 (1913),
295. Traditional pedigrees of various Irish septs are also
given in editions such as Toirdhealbhach Ó
Raithbheartaigh, *Genealogical Tracts* (1932); and Tadhg
Ó Donnchadha, *An Leabhar Muimhneach* (1940). An
edition by Nollaig Ó Muraile is forthcoming of the
Book of Genealogies compiled from old sources by the
17th-century scholar, Dubhaltach Mac Fir Bhisigh.

A large number of pedigrees, compiled since the
16th century, are in GO. For the early 17th century, the

Above: Consulting the
inscriptions of gravestones
where family members are
known to be buried can be
a fruitful exercise in
drawing up the family tree.

Left: The reading room of
the National Library of
Ireland, Dublin.

Calendar of Irish Patent Rolls of James I (published by IMC in 1966) gives the names of persons to whom land was granted by that king. For 1612–13, there is a list of 'Undertakers' i.e. English and Scottish landlords who were granted land in the Ulster Plantation (published in *The Historical Manuscripts Commission Reports*, vol. 4). For 1630 and 1642, the Muster Rolls name large landlords in Ulster and able-bodied men on whom they could call to fight (copies are in the NLI and the Public Record Office of Northern Ireland, Belfast [PRONI]).

Below: The start of the official pedigree of the O'Neills, housed at the Genealogical Office in Dublin.

For 1641 and 1681 there are the *Books of Survey and Distribution* i.e. an English Government list of land ownership for distribution after confiscation. This material—from which the results from County Meath are lacking—is in NAI, with microfilm copies in NLI

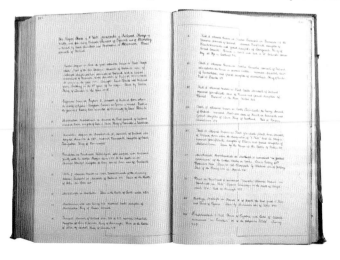

and transcripts in the Royal Irish Academy, Dublin (RIA). The books for Counties Roscommon, Mayo, Galway and Clare have been published by the Irish Manuscripts Commission (IMC). For 1641 to 1698, *Lists of Outlaws* consist of over 6,000 names of people outlawed whose lands were confiscated—microfilm copies of an abstract are in NLI.

For 1654, the *Civil Survey of Ireland* (published by IMC in 3 volumes in 1931), covers Counties Tipperary, Limerick, Waterford, Meath, Donegal and Derry, with incomplete entries for Counties Kerry, Dublin, Kildare, Wexford and Tyrone. It lists the landlords of each town-land and their predecessors in 1641. For 1654, the *Down Survey* gives names of landowners and their religion (published by the Irish Archaeological Society in 1851). For 1659, there is a census of most counties, compiled by Sir William Petty (published by IMC in 1931, ed. Seamus Pender, *The Census of Ireland*).

For 1662 to 1666 Subsidy Rolls are principally concerned with Ulster. They list the nobility, clergy and laity who paid grants in aid to King Charles II. Some of these rolls are in NAI and PRONI, with transcripts in the Representative Church Body Library, Dublin (RCBL). For 1664 to 1666, Hearth Money Rolls give the name of each householder whose dwelling had a hearth. Copies of various of these are in GO, NAI, NLI, PRONI and RCBL.

For 1689 and 1690, information on Irish Jacobites is given by John D'Alton in *Illustrations Historical and Genealogical of King James II's Irish Army List* (published in 1689, and reissued in 1861); and in ed. C. E. Lart, *The Pedigrees and Papers of James Terry 1690–1725* (1938). For 1703, the Convert Rolls list Roman Catholics who changed their religion to the Church of

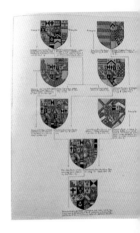

Above: A page from the Book of the Boyles, with the various families represented heraldically.

Ireland (published in IMC Reports in 1981, ed. Eileen O'Byrne). For 1740, there is a list of Protestant householders in several Ulster counties available in GO.

A large number of legal deeds, from 1708 onwards, are registered with indexes in the Registry of Deeds, Dublin (RD). Newspapers began in Ireland in the early 18th century. Good collections of them are held in NLI. Names and addresses of persons engaged in business are in the various directories which were published from the mid 18th century onwards. The best collections of these directories are in NAI and NLI.

Only people of substance made wills, but much information can be gleaned from them. A huge collection of wills, dating from 1536 to 1900, was destroyed in a fire in the Public Record Office of Ireland, Dublin (PROI) in 1922, but copies, abstracts, or indexes of over 60 per cent of them survive in NAI. There are also substantial holdings in GO, NLI and PRONI. Some of the material has been published in journals, and by Sir Arthur Vicars, *Index to the Prerogative Wills of Ireland 1536-1810* (Dublin, 1897).

Below: Only people of substance made wills, but much information can be gleaned from them.

There are fragments of Roman Catholic parish records dating from the late 17th century, but the first appreciable collections are much later —beginning variously in the later 18th century and the 19th century. They contain details of baptisms and of marriages. Microfilm copies of almost all this material are in NLI, but diocesan permission is required to consult some of it. Church of Ireland (Protestant) registers began earlier—some as early as the mid 17th century. Most of its parish registers up to 1871 were destroyed by

Above: Birth certificates are housed at the General Register Office in Dublin.

fire in the PROI in 1922, but RCBL—where the Church of Ireland archives are preserved—has worked admirably to restore the losses. Some records of Presbyterian congregations also date to the 17th century, but registers were not comprehensively undertaken until the 19th century. Microfilms of most of these registers from Northern Ireland until 1900 are in PRONI, whereas most from the rest of Ireland are in local custody. Copies of Methodist and Quaker records are also kept in PRONI. Good lists for clergymen of all denominations are on microfilm in NLI, some of them reaching back to the early 18th century.

For 1775–76, there is a list of Roman Catholics from various counties who took the Oath of Allegiance to the king of England (published in the *59th Report of the Deputy Keeper* of PROI). For 1778–93, Catholic Qualification Rolls list other Roman Catholics who took the Oath. An index to it—containing names, occupations, dates and places—survives in NAI.

Above: For 1796 a Spinning-Wheel Entitlement gives the names of persons who received spinning wheels as part of a government scheme.

For 1795, the Charter Trust Fund Marriage Certificates in NAI list Protestant labourers in north Leinster and County Cavan who were given small gratuities on marriage. For 1796, a Spinning Wheel Entitlement gives by district the names of persons—almost 60,000 in all, mostly in Ulster—who received free spinning wheels through a government scheme to encourage the linen trade. Indexes to the list are in NAI and PRONI. Details from two interesting local census survive—one from Elphin Diocese in 1749 (in NAI); and one for the town of Carrick-on-Suir in 1799 (microfilm copy in NLI).

For 1823 to 1838, the Tithe Applotment Books, and related material for all Ireland, specify the amount of money to be paid by each landholder to the Church of Ireland. Poor people also had to pay these tithes. The originals are in NAI; with microfilm copies in NLI and (for the nine Ulster counties) in PRONI. For 1848 to 1864, the Valuation of Ireland was carried out under the direction of Richard Griffith (published at the time by the General Valuation Office, Dublin [GVO], as *The Valuation of Ireland*). Householders' names are listed by

Below: Irish peasantry. Tithes fell most heavily on the poor.

county, barony, parish and townland. The surnames which occur in this source and in the Tithe Applotments are arranged by parish in a combined index, copies of which are in NLI, NAI, PRONI and GO. Less extensive revaluation books, covering the period down to 1929, are in GVO and PRONI. From 1837 to 1896, the

Incumbered Estate Records, with details concerning the estates of bankrupt landlords, are preserved in NLI. For 1876, *Landowners in Ireland* (published officially in London in 1876) gives a list of the 32,614 persons—identified by province and county—who owned land exceeding an acre in that year.

Of great value are the National School Records for 1831 to 1921, which give the name, age and religion of each pupil, as well as the parents' address and occupation. PRONI has most of these registers for the six northern counties, but for the other 26 counties the school records are still kept locally. From 1838 to 1848, the Poor Law Records give details of inmates of workhouses and infirmaries—parts survive and are available in NAI, PRONI and county libraries. With the introduction of the Old Age Pension scheme in 1908, much information was assembled concerning the claimants and their families—these records are preserved in NAI and PRONI. Much more comprehensively, the General Register Office, Dublin (GRO) has

Below: Irish schoolgirls in the 1890s. National school records are of great value in tracing your genealogy.

Above: A 19th-century workhouse. Poor Law records can provide details of inmates of workhouses between 1838 and 1848.

Right: A cartoon satirising the policies which caused large numbers of people to emigrate from Ireland.

records of all births, marriages, and deaths, from 1864 for all counties up to 1921, and for the 26 counties of the Republic thereafter. For the six northern counties after 1921, these records are held in The Register General, Belfast (RG).

There are also other lists and valuations, variously kept in GO, NAI, NLI, PRONI, TCD and other locations. These include local lists of freeholders compiled from the 17th century onwards. From the same period are miscellaneous voters' lists and poll-tax books. More comprehensive are the lists of, and files on, state prisoners and convicted persons, covering the period 1788 to 1868, in the State Paper Office, Dublin (SPO). Militia and army lists from 1750 onwards are preserved variously in GO, NLI, PRONI and the Public Record Office at Kew in Surrey, England. Details of policemen for all of Ireland, from 1816 to 1922, are kept in microfiche copies in NAI and PRONI.

The most efficient method of tracing relatives would be from census reports; however, the material available is very unsatisfactory. A full census of Ireland was taken every ten years from 1821 to 1911, but only

Left: A sketch of a man taking a census around 1870. A full census of Ireland was taken every ten years from 1821 to 1911, but only fragments of these records remain.

fragments of these records remain. Now in NAI, they are as follows: 1821 (partially for Counties Cavan, Fermanagh, Galway, Meath and Offaly); 1831 (partially for County Derry); 1841 (Killeshandra in County Cavan only); 1851 (partial, mostly from County Antrim). In addition, some transcripts and abstracts made from the original 1841 to 1891 returns have been found. This means that the earliest comprehensive returns which survive come from the census taken in 1901 and 1911, kept in NAI. Copies of the 1901 returns for the six counties of Northern Ireland are also available at PRONI. No census was taken in 1921, and subsequent census are subject to a 100-year closure.

Derived from several of the above-mentioned sources is the Irish section of the *International Genealogical Index*, compiled by the Church of Jesus Christ of Latter-Day Saints (CLDS) and available in their major repositories. For detailed information on sources and how to consult them, see John Grenham, *Tracing Your Irish Ancestors* (Dublin, 1999).

THE RYANS

SEANCHAS RIANACH

THERE ARE TWO DIFFERENT SEPTS
BEARING THE SURNAME RYAN, BUT
BOTH ARE OF THE SAME ORIGIN, BEING
DESCENDED FROM EARLY KINGS OF
LEINSTER. ONE SEPT BELONGS TO
COUNTY CARLOW, AND THE OTHER TO
COUNTIES TIPPERARY AND LIMERICK.
THEIR LATIN MOTTO IS *MALO MORI
QUAM FOEDARI* ('I WOULD PREFER TO
DIE THAN TO BE DISGRACED').

THE ORIGINS

The prestigious kingdom of Tara in prehistoric Ireland was held for a while by the Laighin (Leinstermen), and their cultus at that site involved the Celtic title Catuveros ('battle-man') for their king. Long after they had lost Tara, these Leinstermen preserved the memory of the cultus, supposing that the title Catuveros—which had become Cathaoir—was actually the name of a great king of theirs who had ruled at Tara.

It was further claimed that the youngest son of Cathaoir, called Fiacha Baicidh, gained his father's blessing together with a promise that his descendants would be the most important of the Leinstermen. The son of Fiacha Baicidh, Breasal Béalach, king of Leinster, refused to pay tribute to the great Uí Néill kings of Tara. When the Uí Néill attacked his province in retaliation, Breasal is reputed to have defeated them in battle at Cnámhros (Camross in County Laois). From the first son of this Breasal Béalach, Éanna Nia, are descended families such as the Byrnes and O'Tooles. The second son was Labhraidh Láidheach, who in turn had three sons—Éanna Cinsealach, Drón, and Daigh. Éanna Cinsealach succeeded his grandfather as king of the Leinstermen, and he was in turn succeeded by his son Criomhthann, who died in or about 483 AD. Criomhthann's son, named Nath Í, did not gain the Leinster kingship, though several of his posterity did.

One of the sons of Nath Í, apparently the senior, was Eoghan Caoch ('Eoghan the One-Eyed'), who was ancestor of the MacMurroughs, Kavanaghs, and Kinsellas. Another son was Cormac, and his progeny

Left: The Glen of Aherlow is an important pass between Counties Tipperary and Limerick. There are two different septs bearing the surname Ryan. One belongs to Tipperary and Limerick, the other to County Carlow.

were known as Síol Chormaic. Rónán, grandson of Cormac, became king of Leinster and died around the year 624. His son again, Crunnmhaol (656) was also king of the province. Crunnmhaol's son, Aodh Rón, did not attain to the Leinster kingship, but was an important figure in the province's public life.

Towards the end of the eighth century, the descendants of Aodh Rón gained a sub-kingdom of their own in the centre of Leinster territory. This had previously belonged to far-out relatives of theirs, the progeny of Drón, brother of Éanna Cinsealach. The kingdom was therefore called Uí Dhróna, and is the area covered by the two baronies called in English 'Idrone', which form the western part of modern County Carlow. In the

Below: The Hill of Tara in County Meath. An ancient settlement steeped in mythological history, this was the seat of the high-kings of Ireland.

Left: The Rawlinson B 502 manuscript, now in the Bodleian Library, Oxford, England, is the earliest Irish manuscript to contain genealogical material, in this case about the kings of Leinster.

tenth century, the lord of Idrone—eighth in direct descent from Aodh Rón—was Rian. Many interpretations have been offered for the name of this chieftain, but its real meaning must be 'the kingly man'. His two sons succeeded him as chieftain, Muireadhach and Cairbre. The latter had three sons, one of whom, Tadhg, became chieftain with the title *ua Riain* ('grandson of Rian'), the origin of the surname Ó Rian.

Right: County Carlow. Towards the end of the eighth century the descendants of Aedh Rón gained a sub-kingdom of their own in the centre of Leinster territory. Called Uí Dhróna, this was the area covered by the two baronies called in English 'Idrone', which form the western part of modern County Carlow.

Tadhg is mentioned in the annals in a tragic context. We read that, in the year 1016, he and Donn Cuain, king of Leinster, were slain by Donnchadh Mac Giolla Phádraig at Tadhg's dwelling in Leighlin, 'after they had made friendship and taken an oath together in the beginning of the day'. This treachery by Mac Giolla Phádraig, lord of Ossory, was part of a longstanding conflict between Leinster and the men of Ossory (modern Kilkenny and south Laois) who were not of the same stock as the Leinstermen. The Ó Riain lords of Idrone bordered directly on Ossory, and Tadhg was obviously attempting to make peace between the warring parties. It was claimed at the time that this murder had been prophesied long before by the famous Leinster saint, Moling, who also foretold that much bloodshed would follow.

Bloodshed there was, for the high-king of Ireland, Maol Seachnaill II, brought his large army south and slew Mac Giolla Phádraig. Among the deaths reported was that of one Dubh Dábhoireann Ó Riain, no doubt a close relative of the murdered Tadhg, whose successor in the lordship of Idrone was his son, Donnchadh. He in turn was succeeded by Maol Seachnaill Ó Riain— the occurrence of this name in the family (in later form Maoilsheachlainn, or Malachy) may be due to the intervention of the high-king in the sept's favour.

When the first Norman forces landed in Ireland these Ryans joined the effort to repel them. This was a remarkable act of independence, for the Normans had been brought to the country by the Leinster king, Diarmaid MacMurrough, who belonged to the same basic stock of Éanna Cinsealach. The Normans had seized Waterford city in 1170, and the Ryans sent a force south to combine with the ruling sept of that area, the Phelans, lords of the Déise. It was the first resistance to the invaders offered by the Irish, but the Ryans and Phelans were defeated with great slaughter. About 500 prisoners were taken by the Normans, and these were cruelly massacred.

The resistance continued, however, and when the Norman leader, Richard de Clare

Above: The Anglo-Norman FitzStephen, sent by Strongbow to pacify Ireland, burns his boats off the coast of Wexford, as a sign that he has no intention of retreating. When the Normans first arrived in Ireland, the Ryans joined the effort to repel them.

Left: King Henry II of England at Waterford.

('Strongbow'), marched his army through Idrone, he was ambushed by the Ryans. At the height of the fighting the chieftain, Diarmaid Ó Riain, was shot dead by an arrow, after which his men fled. Following on this, most of the Ryan country was given to the Norman captain, Raymond le Gros, and his Irish allies, the MacMurroughs. The latter gave back some of the territory to the Ryans to hold as clients, however. When, in the 13th century, the MacMurroughs began to reassert their premier claim over the Anglo-Normans, they further strengthened the Ryans, whose new base was in Ballyellin, east of the river Barrow.

Above: The seal of the Norman leader Strongbow. Below: The reputed tomb of Strongbow, who died in 1176, in Christchurch Cathedral, Dublin.

In that place, the family name became synonymous with prestige and hospitality. Poets of the 14th century referred to their chieftain as 'Ó Riain, king of Idrone, the very bravest' and 'Ó Riain, to whom belonged the long cantred of Idrone among the pleasant hills'.

THE MULRYANS

Similar origins in early Leinster are attributed to the sept which was known by the surname Ó Maoilriain (anglicised as Mulryan). In their official genealogy (which was compiled in the 16th century) the Mulryans claimed descent—not from Cormac—but from the other son of Nath Í, Eoghan Caoch. This genealogy traces them from a son of Eoghan Caoch called Fearghus, but such a Fearghus is not mentioned in any other source. That Fearghus and the Eoghan Caoch attribution are inventions, is borne out by the fact that otherwise the early part of the Mulryan genealogy is a duplicate of the pedigree of the Ryans of Idrone.

There is good reason, however, for taking seriously the definite claim to Leinster ancestry and the connection with the namesake sept. The eponym, Maoilrian, comes from an earlier form, Mael Riain, which meant literally 'servant/devotee of Rian'. Bearing in mind the official Mulryan genealogy, the suggestion must be that the Rian in question was the same man as the ancestor of the Ryans of Idrone. It is possible that the personage Mael Riain was a relative of Rian, but the greater probability is that he was a member of a kindred Leinster sept which supported Rian. Perhaps he even belonged to the old Uí Dhróna sept, which had become assimilated to the Ryan line of Síol Chormaic.

After their invasion in 1169, the Normans quickly spread their power throughout Leinster and Munster. The rich lands of central Munster were particularly attractive to them; and in that region—to the south-east of the river Shannon—lay a district called Uaithne, stretching from the Silvermines mountains to Tower

Right: The river Shannon. After their invasion in 1169, the Normans quickly spread their power throughout Leinster and Munster. The rich lands of central Munster were particularly attractive to them.

Hill. Uaithne was the name of an ancient tribe inhabiting that district, which straddles the Tipperary-Limerick border and is known in English as the barony of 'Owney'. As early as 1186, King John granted the whole of North Tipperary (called Urmhumhain, or Ormond) to Theobald Walter, ancestor of the Butlers. He also granted wide territory further south along the Tipperary-Limerick border to William de Burgo, which territory was later known as Clanwilliam.

Apart from the construction of some fortifications and castles, the grants did not have a major immediate impact on these areas. The most important event in Owney was the building of a small Cistercian monastery there early in the 13th century, which became known as Abington. Norman power gradually grew, however, leading to increasing tension. In 1283 Owney was seized by the combined forces of Toirdhealbhach Ó Briain, native king of north Munster, and the Norman Thomas de Clare. This must have caused the age-old inhabitants of Owney—Lynches, Heffernans, and Culhanes—to be dispossessed of much of their lands. After the death of Thomas de Clare in 1287, the powerful Norman lords, the Butlers and de Burgos, attempted to make real their claims on the area.

In 1297 the earl of Ulster, Richard de Burgo, is reported as giving security for the Dwyers and the Mulryans. The Dwyers were the native inhabitants of the barony of Kilnamanagh, which borders on Owney to the south-east. The son of Richard de Burgo, Edmund, became lord of Clanwilliam, which lies to the

Left: Ormond Castle, dating from the 14th century belonged to the great Norman family the Butlers.

Right: Coat of arms of the Norman family the Burkes. The Mulryans of Clonoulty showed a strong Norman connection, demonstrated by the occurrence of the first name 'William', a favourite of the de Burgo (later Burke) family.

south of Kilnamanagh. It is clear from the occurrence of the Mulryans in this context that they were already in the region, and in 1305 several of the Mulryan family are reported at Clonoulty, in the middle of Kilnamanagh. The names given were William Buí ('the Sallow'), Tadhg Carrach, Diarmaid Liath and Maoilsheachlainn, all apparently leading men of their sept, and all, except for William, having names established among the Ryans of Idrone. These Mulryans of Clonoulty were listed as supporters of the Knights Templars, which shows a strong Norman connection. The occurrence of the name William among them is also significant, as it was a Norman one and a favourite in the de Burgo (later, Burke) family.

In their official genealogy, the Mulryans claimed that their ancestor, 'the son of Rian', had been called William. We have seen, however, that this Rian lived in the tenth century, and the name William would not have been used in Ireland at that time. It would therefore appear that the Mulryans had moved from their Carlow homeland in the mid 13th century and that they had been assisted in this move by the powerful de Burgo family. The other major Norman family in the region, the Butlers, held lands stretching right across Counties Tipperary and Kilkenny, into County Carlow. As it was a common practice for the Norman overlords to encourage native groups to resettle in different areas as 'marcher' communities, the movement of a group from County Carlow to County Tipperary would not be unusual at the time.

To judge by the genealogy, William Ó Maoilriain was the first leader of the transferred sept, and he was succeeded by his son and grandson, both called by the ancient Leinster name of Cairbre. The son of the latter, William Buí, was probably the man referred to at Clonoulty in or about 1306. Some of them remained in that area, where they established a strong centre at Kilnalongurty, ten kilometres to the north. A generation

Left: Cahir Castle, Co. Tipperary, dates from the 13th century, and was owned by the powerful Butler family.

or two later, the major section of the family had spread west and was established at Owney, where they multiplied and became quite powerful. Their chieftains for the next 100 years were Conchobhar, Conchobhar Lochlann, Donncha Mór, Donncha Cam, Lorcán and Dónall.

By 1436, the Mulryans of Owney felt themselves strong enough to demand that a native Irish abbot be appointed to the old Butler foundation of Abington. Dónall's son, Conchobhar (which name was by then pronounced 'Conchúr'), installed as abbot Diarmaid Ó Glasáin, and the Anglo-Norman monks of the abbey complained of this to James Butler, fourth earl of Ormond. They claimed that Dónall and his son were trying to force their compliance with the new Irish abbot by denying them provisions and even curtailing their right to travel outside the monastic grounds. Some sort of compromise was probably reached, but the principle that an Irishman could be abbot had been established by the Mulryans.

Below: A 15th-century monk copies a manuscript.

Conchúr, who succeeded his father, Dónall, was a very independent spirit and, in order to curb him, the earl of Ormond combined forces with the sixth earl of Desmond, James FitzGerald, in 1452. They attacked the castle of Owney, where Conchúr lived, and destroyed it; but Conchúr hit back immediately by ambushing Maurice, the son of the Desmond earl. Maurice's

horse was wounded and fell, killing the young Geraldine. Soon after, the sons of both earls gave battle to Conchúr, in which the latter's two sons and many of his followers were slain. Conchúr himself escaped on his fine horse, but he was later cut to pieces by the enemy.

The ecclesiastical ambitions of the family were not to be denied, however. In 1455 Mathúin Ó Maoilriain was abbot of the great abbey of Holycross in County Tipperary, and several of the Mulryans were in charge of other churches in County Tipperary when King Henry VIII suppressed the monasteries. Among these was Abington itself, the abbot of which at that time was Seán Ó Maoilriain. Seán was allowed to hold on to the site as a secular provost.

Above: Holycross Abbey, Co. Tipperary. In 1455 Mathúin Ó Maoilriain was abbot here, and several of the Mulryans were in charge of other churches in County Tipperary.

CENTURIES OF TURBULENCE

Right: King Henry VIII of England.

The chieftain who oversaw the aforementioned situation and prevented the wrath of Henry VIII from descending on his territory was Diarmaid Ó Maoilriain, great-grandson of that Conchúr who had fought against the Butlers and Geraldines. Diarmaid was of an equally independent disposition. In 1538 he put a pledge of cows into the hands of James FitzGerald, 12th earl of Desmond, for a debt of 40 marks. Having paid the debt, he sought his cows back. The earl refused, and Diarmaid prepared for a fight, but the earl was advised by friends to restore the cattle. Relations were soon repaired, for in the following year Diarmaid supported the Desmond earl when the lord deputy for Ireland, Lord Leonard Grey, launched an offensive against Fitzgerald. When the large English army approached Owney, Diarmaid wisely submitted and, in 1540—with the title of 'Captain of the country of Owney'—he agreed to supply 60 Gallowglasses (hired fighters) to the king's service.

Diarmaid's shrewd policy did not long survive him, however, and the Mulryans, almost to a man, were involved in the great rebellion of the earl of Desmond which began in 1579. Even though the Butlers of Ormond were to the fore on the government side, it is interesting to note that most of the Burkes of Clanwilliam, old associates of the Mulryans, and relatives of theirs through several marriages, joined wholeheartedly in the rebellion. A major role was played by the curate of Owney, Conchúr Ó Maoilriain (Cornelius Mulryan), who had been appointed bishop of Killaloe in 1576 and then transferred to the See of Cork. He went to Rome and Spain in an attempt to organise an expeditionary force for Ireland in support of the rebellion. Bad luck dogged his tracks, and he determined to return home in 1582, but was captured by pirates off La Rochelle. He escaped, remaining abroad until his death in 1596. Another member of the sept, Henry Mulryan, was an officer in a large expeditionary fleet sailing from Spain to Ireland, which was

Below: An Irish Gallowglass of the 16th century. When a large English army approached Owney, Diarmaid Ó Maoilriain, wisely submitted and agreed to supply 60 Gallowglasses to King Henry VIII's service.

Right: Sir George Carew, English soldier and statesman. In 1600 he led an army into Owney, burning the countryside and slaughtering both young and old.

wrecked off the Cabo de Fisterra in 1596.

The Mulryan chieftain at this time was Conchúr, grandson of Diarmaid. He led his people in support of the Desmond rebellion and of the rebellion of the Ulster princes which followed. As a result, Sir George Carew led an English army into Owney in 1600, burning all the countryside and slaughtering both young and old. A few years later most of the Mulryan-held land was confiscated. A tombstone in Abington cemetery marks the grave of William, the last official chieftain of the Mulryan sept, who died in 1632.

The Mulryans were still very numerous in that whole area, however, and they played an active role in the campaign against Oliver Cromwell when Owney was again attacked and Abington destroyed in 1647. In the Cromwellian plantation of 1655, all the Mulryans in the baronies of Owney, Ara, Clanwilliam, and Kilnamanagh were dispossessed and their lands given to Cromwellian soldiers and financiers. Dozens of their most extensive landowners were forcibly transplanted west across the Shannon. Some returned later, to join the many other Mulryans in

Above: Oliver Cromwell, the English soldier and statesman. The Mulryans played an active role in the campaign against his brutal tactics in Ireland.

Left: One of Cromwell's light horsemen.

much reduced circumstances. From this time onwards, they tended to simplify their surname from Ó Maoilriain (Mulryan) to Ó Riain (Ryan). The precise reason for this is unclear, but—in ordinary speech at any rate—the pronunciations of the two surnames were very similar, Ó Riain being spoken as 'o ree-en' and Ó Maoilriain as 'o mree-en'.

In County Carlow, the fortunes of the Ryan sept, more properly so called, were not very different. Since they also joined in repeated rebellions by the native Irish, almost all of their territory in Idrone was confiscated. A story is told that, after

the death of the chieftain, Donncha Ó Riain, in 1625, his house in Ballyellin was taken from his children, and the new occupants found a pot full of gold—the family heirloom—buried under a kitchen slab. One branch of these Ryans did retain their property, after two of them died for the cause of King William of Orange in the Battle of the Boyne in 1690. Thus Anthony Ryan had an estate in Haroldstown, and his two sons had lands at Broghillstown and Leighlinbridge.

Most of the Ryans supported James II, and, f

Right: William III, Prince of Orange and king of England.

ollowing the Treaty of Limerick in 1691, many of them joined Continental armies. Of those in the French service, the highest ranked was Lieutenant-Colonel James Patrick O'Mulryan, born in 1716, who fought against the Turks in 1739–49 and the Prussians in 1756–63, and was decorated for bravery at the Siege of Schweidnitz in 1747. Captain Luke Ryan was an officer in the Irish Brigade of the French army, who went on to command a privateer ship during the American War of Independence. He was captured by the English and sentenced to execution three times at the Old Bailey in London, but was reprieved at the insistence of the French. He had amassed a fortune, but lost it all in banking ventures and died in a debtor's prison in 1789.

Cornelius O'Ryan from Gortenossy, near Ballingarry in County Tipperary, was an Irish officer who went

Above: William III at the Battle of the Boyne where he defeated James II. Some Ryans fought and died for the cause of King William, but most supported King James.

Above: The Siege of Limerick in 1691. Following the Treaty of Limerick, many Ryans went abroad where they became officers in the Spanish, French and Austrian armies.

abroad after the defeat of 1691. He joined the French and Spanish armies, and was killed in the Battle of Almanza in 1707. Among his descendants was Gabriel O'Ryan, governor of Havana in 1816. Lieutenant-General Tomás O'Ryan (1821–1902), was descended directly from the Mulryans of Owney—he was a leading engineer in the Spanish army, fought in the Crimean War, became tutor to the young King Alfonso XII, and served for a while as Spanish minister for war.

A man who kept the original form of his surname was William O'Mulryan of Thurles, who settled near Barcelona. His grandson, Ignacio O'Mulryan, became a knight in the order of King Carlos III of Spain and minister of the Royal Council of the Indies. Several other members of that family were distinguished soldiers. One of them, Brigadier-General Fernando O'Mulryan (1840–1906), was commander of the Cortes regiment of cavalry in the Cuban war against the USA in 1897. His nephew, José O'Mulryan (1874–1928), was decorated for his part in that war, and later served as lieutenant-colonel in the Spanish army in Africa.

Of the Irishmen who did not go abroad, but remained at home as 'raparees' (outlaws carrying out raids on the planters), the most famous was Éamonn Ó Maoilriain, a native of Knockmeoll in the centre of County Tipperary. He belonged to the Kilnalongurty family. Known as *Éamonn an Chnoic* ('Ned of the Hill'), he was proclaimed an outlaw in 1702 with the then enormous price of £200 on his head. Folklore claims that he first took to outlawry when he saw the only cow of a poor widow being seized by a land-agent. He attacked the agent, who was killed in the struggle. The red-coat soldiers, stationed at Borrisoleigh, were sent to arrest him, but he repeatedly outsmarted and outfought them. He was a splendid horseman and swordsman, and was very accurate with his brace of pistols.

It is said that he once encountered a rich English lady who had been robbed, and that he regained her

Below: The Battle of Almanza. Cornelius O'Ryan, who went abroad after the Treaty of Limerick in 1691, died here in 1707.

Above: The Crimean War. Tomás O'Ryan fought in this campaign.

Below: A verse from the Irish love-song, *Éamonn an Chnoic*.

> 'Oh who is without
> That with passionate shout
> Keeps beating my bolted door?'
> 'I am Ned of the Hill
> Forspent wet and chill
> From long trudging
> marsh and moor.'
> 'My love, fond and true
> What else could I do
> But shield you from wind and from weather?
> When the shots fall like hail
> They us both shall assail
> And mayhap we shall die together.'

money for her. She was the wife of an English army officer, and she determined to get a pardon for Éamonn. She succeeded, but before it was proclaimed, he was betrayed and beheaded by a relative who wished to collect the reward for his capture. One of the best-known Irish love-songs, *Éamonn an Chnoic*, was reputedly composed by him for a girl called Mary Leahy.

Another soldier who stayed at home was Tadhg Ó Maoilriain or Thaddeus Ryan of Ballyvistea, a cavalry-officer in the Jacobite army. Despite the confiscations, he managed to hold on to his lands at Ballvistea and Scarteen, near Knocklong in County Limerick. The name Thaddeus or 'Thady' was a recurrent one among his descendants, many of whom were renowned huntsmen. Major-General Thaddeus Richard Ryan (1837–1905), seems to have been the originator of the famed Scarteen Foxhounds, of which his heirs have been master to the present day.

MODERN TIMES

A number of Ryans have become prominent political and business figures. Daniel F. Ryan (1762–98), born in County Wexford, was a strong loyalist and editor of the *Dublin Journal*. He was part of the police party which arrested the famous republican Lord Edward Fitzgerald in 1798. During this incident there was a struggle and both men were killed.

US financier Thomas 'Fortune' Ryan (1851–1928) played a key role in numerous business organisations at the turn of the 20th century. He died leaving a fortune of over $200 million!

Frank Ryan (1902–44), born in County Limerick, fought in the War of Independence and became an Irish Republican Army leader. He then recruited 200 Irish volunteers for the International Brigade during the Spanish Civil War. He was captured during the fighting and sentenced to death. A nationwide campaign in Ireland to save his life led to his sentence being commuted to 30 years' imprisonment. He was then taken to Germany in 1940 where the Nazis hoped he would join their war effort. He refused and eventually died in a Dresden sanatorium.

Thelma Ryan (1912–93), born in Nevada, married Richard Nixon who became US president in 1969. As First Lady she opened the White House to many special needs groups and directed a

Below: A Spanish Civil War poster for the International Brigade. Frank Ryan recruited 200 Irish volunteers for the Brigade.

Above: American president Richard Nixon and the First Lady, formerly Thelma Ryan.

Right: The ever-popular Barbie doll, developed by inventor Jack Ryan.

major refurbishment. She was nicknamed Pat as she was born on the eve of St. Patrick's Day.

Eccentric US inventor Jack Ryan (1926–91) joined toy manufacturer Mattel Inc. in 1955. He became a multimillionaire by developing some 35 best-selling toys, including the ever-popular Barbie doll.

Businessman Tony Ryan (1936–), founded Ryanair in 1985. It first operated a daily flight from Waterford to London Gatwick. In 1986 it began the Dublin to London route. It is now Europe's largest low-cost airline, carrying over 12 million people per annum to destinations across Europe.

A number of Ryans have become prominent in the arts and media. US priest Abraham Ryan (1838–86) served as a Confederate chaplain in the American Civil War. The Confederate defeat and the death of his

brother in action moved him to write a series of poems. Many of his verses became household favourites, several were set to music, and he became the recognised poet of the Confederacy.

Left: American actor Robert Ryan appeared in over 70 films.

American actor Robert Ryan (1909–73), became one of cinema's best 'bad guys'. He established his reputation playing the Oscar-nominated role of an anti-Semitic bully in *Crossfire* (1947). He went on to appear in over 70 films, many of them Westerns or crime dramas.

Cornelius Ryan (1920–74), born in Dublin, was a war journalist who covered D-Day, the advance of General Patton's third army in Europe (1944–45). His book *The Longest Day* (1959), based on the Normandy invasion, became a best-seller and was made into a film. *The Last Battle* (1960) on Berlin in 1945, and *A Bridge Too Far* (1974) on the Arnhem operation, each sold several million copies.

John Ryan (1925–92), born in Dublin, was a writer, broadcaster and publican who also became one of the leading Irish artists of his time. He produced many fine portraits, historical scenes and sensitive still-life paintings.

The English singer Marion Ryan appeared on the

Below: A scene from the film *The Longest Day*, starring Henry Fonda and adapted from Cornelius Ryan's novel of the same name.

music scene in 1953 and soon became a favourite on shows such as the *6.5 Special* and featured in Tommy Steele's movie, *It's All Happening* (1963). Her twin sons, Paul and Barry (1948–), released their debut single in 1965, and Paul later achieved a number two hit with 'Eloise'.

US actress Meg Ryan (1961–) found fame with a supporting role in the blockbuster *Top Gun* (1986). This led to lead roles in *Inner Space* (1987), *When Harry Met Sally* (1989), and *Sleepless in Seattle* (1993).

David Lean's movie *Ryan's Daughter* (1970) tells the compelling story of Rosy Ryan (Sarah Miles), the daughter of an Irish politician during the First World War who falls in love with a British officer. Steven Spielberg's blockbuster *Saving Private Ryan* (1996) recounts the story of a dangerous US infantry mission

Above: The English singer Marion Ryan, and her twin sons, Paul and Barry.

Right: American actress Meg Ryan made her name with a supporting role in the US blockbuster *Top Gun*.

to rescue fictional character Private James Ryan (Matt Damon) during the Normandy campaign (1944). The plot was actually inspired by a family called Niland from New York State.

Several sporting heroes also bear the name. US

boxer Tommy Ryan (1878–1948) assumed the name after he began boxing in 1887. He became welterweight champion in 1894 and also successfully boxed as a middleweight. He fought 104 fights but only had three official defeats.

Patrick J. Ryan (1883–1964), born in County Limerick, was an Olympic hammer-throwing champion who emigrated to the United States and set a world record in 1913 which stood until 1937. He won his Olympic Gold medal at Antwerp in 1920.

US baseball pitcher Nolan Ryan (1947–) was signed by the New York Mets aged 18, and began major league play in 1968. He became the first pitcher to surpass Walter Johnson's record of 3,508 strikeouts set in 1927, and held the record for most strikeouts in a season (383 in 1973). He is the oldest pitcher ever to lead a major league in strikeouts (in 1989 at the age of 42), and finally retired in 1993.

Above: American boxer Tommy Ryan had 104 fights, but only three official defeats.

Left: The American baseball pitcher Nolan Ryan had a long career in the game, spanning 28 years.

Charles A. Lindbergh made the first non-stop solo flight from New York to Paris (1927) in the *Spirit of St. Louis*, a Ryan NYP developed from the Ryan M2. The single-engine, high-wing monoplane, modified to Lindbergh's specifications, was donated to the Smithsonian Institution.

The family's military heroes include four holders of the Victoria Cross, Britain's top gallantry award. John Ryan of the 1st Madras Fusiliers and Miles Ryan of the European Bengal Fusiliers won their medals during the Indian Mutiny (1857). John Ryan of the 65th Regiment won the medal in New Zealand (1863), and John Ryan of the Australian Imperial Force won the medal on the Western Front (1918). The prestigious US Congressional Medal of Honor was won by Thomas Ryan during the Boxer Rebellion in China (1900). Admiral Thomas J. Ryan won the medal saving a woman from a burning hotel during the 1923 Yokohama earthquake in Japan.

Less acclaimed for his actions was the infamous criminal (Frank) Chew Tobacco Ryan, part of Chicago's infamous Capone gang who were responsible for operating gambling houses and other rackets in the city. Canadian Frank P. Ryan (1942–84) emerged in 1979 as the leader of a powerful drugs network in Montreal. He was murdered in 1984 by French-Canadian mobsters. They in turn were blown up 12 days later in revenge. At

Above: Charles A. Lindbergh made the first non-stop solo flight from New York to Paris in the *Spirit of St. Louis*, a Ryan NYP developed from the Ryan M2.

Above: An aerial view of a farm in Ryan, Iowa, USA.

the time of his death he was worth between $50 and $100 million.

Places bearing the name include two communities in the United States. Ryan (population 382 in 1990) is the name of an agricultural town in Iowa, as well as the name of a town in Oklahoma (population 945 in 1990).

Ryan Loch is a narrow sheltered inlet of the Irish Sea in Dumfries and Galloway in Scotland. It extends nine miles, north to south. Ryan Peak in south central Idaho rises up 11.795ft.

Today the Ryan family are to be found across the world. While they have an ancient and noble ancestry, they still play a major part in many areas of human endeavour around the globe.

Left: US Marines march during the Boxer Rebellion of 1900. The prestigious US Congressional Medal of Honor was won by Thomas Ryan.

PICTURE CREDITS

The publishers are grateful to the individual
photographers and institutions who have made
illustrations available for this book, as follows:

The Art Archive: 50

Chrysalis Books Archive: 1, 6, 8, 9 (top), 9 (bottom),
11, 15 (top), 15 (bottom), 16, 20, 21, 24 (top), 24
(bottom), 28, 30, 32, 33, 34, 36 (top), 36 (bottom),
40, 43, 44, 45, 47 (top), 48, 55

Corbis: 2, 13 (top), 13 (bottom), 14, 18, 19 (top), 19
(bottom), 22, 25, 38, 39, 41, 51, 53, 54 (top), 54
(bottom), 59 (top), 60 (top), 60 (bottom), 61

Mary Evans Picture Library: 10, 26 (top), 34
(bottom), 35, 42, 49

Hulton|Archive: 12, 26 (bottom), 27, 46, 47
(bottom), 56, 58, 59 (bottom)

Rex Features: 57

Antony Shaw: 23, 52